SECOND NATURE
CHANGES & CHALLENGES IN THE NEW ENVIRONMENT

Trash Talk
WHAT YOU THROW AWAY

By Amy Tilmont and Jeff Garside
with Mark Stewart

NORWOOD HOUSE PRESS

All photos courtesy of Getty Images, except for the following:
Deposit Photos (4, 20); National Aeronautics and Space Administration (10, 26); Christopher
Zaborsky (31); TerraCycle (34); Blacksmith Institute (35); Margo Bors (36); Denis Hayes (43).

Front Cover: Deposit Photos

Special thanks to Content Consultant Ashley McDowell.

Library of Congress Cataloging-in-Publication Data

Tilmont, Amy.
  Trash talk : what you throw away / by Amy Tilmont, Jeff Garside, Mark
Stewart.
      p. cm. -- (Second nature)
  Includes bibliographical references and index.
Summary: "This book looks at the waste products humans create and how they
affect the environment. Young readers learn why what you don't see can hurt
you...and also understand the innovative steps they can take now and in the
future to make a difference in meeting the challenges posed by the planet's
garbage crisis"--Provided by publisher.
    ISBN-13: 978-1-59953-459-6 (library edition : alk. paper)
    ISBN-10: 1-59953-459-2 (library edition : alk. paper)
1. Refuse and refuse disposal--Environmental aspects--Juvenile literature.
2. Litter (Trash)--Environmental aspects--Juvenile literature. I. Garside,
Jeff. II. Stewart, Mark, 1960- III. Title.
  TD792.T55 2011
  363.72'8--dc23
                        2011017628

Manufactured in the United States of America in North Mankato, Minnesota.
176N—072011

COVER: Trash disposed of carelessly poses a problem for people around the world.

Contents

Words in **bold type** are defined on page 46.

1 What's the Problem?
TRASH OUT OF CONTROL

Out of sight, out of mind. What does this old saying mean? Once something disappears from view, you don't need to think about it anymore. But when it comes to the things we throw away, nothing could be further from the truth.

We focus a lot of attention on air pollution, **climate change**, and the problems caused by fossil fuels. In doing so, we forget the impact each of us has in our daily lives, as we fill up garbage cans and wastebaskets until it's time to take out the trash. Where exactly is *out*? Where does trash go after it is carted away from our homes, schools, and businesses? It may be out of sight, but it shouldn't be out of mind. Disposing of garbage in a safe way is one of the biggest environmental challenges we face.

On average, people in the United States create 4.4 pounds (2 kilograms) of garbage a day, and every bit of it has to go somewhere. Almost all of it ends up entering the environment in one way or another. Much of the damage done by garbage is permanent. It comes back to us in the air we breathe, the food we eat, and the water we drink. It also puts the plants and animals we depend upon under extreme stress. In the long run, that may be the worst outcome of all.

Will the day come when we have no places left to dispose of our trash?

BURIED AND BURNED

In most developed countries, trash is carted to landfills, where it is buried. This reduces the number of disease-carrying animals that are attracted to garbage. It also keeps trash from blowing away. If a landfill is built correctly, it will keep chemicals in the garbage from entering the surrounding environment.

Composting is another form of "waste management" that is growing in popularity. This is the process of turning **biodegradable** waste into nutrients for soil. Compostable items include things you usually throw away—from fruit and vegetable scraps to leaves and grass. Many people compost on their own, but garbage companies have begun to offer this service to their customers as well.

In many parts of the world, trash is also burned in a process known as **incineration**. This method of disposal reduces the volume of trash by up to 80 percent. It is limited to **organic** material—things such as food and paper, which come from living things. Burning of synthetic material, such as plastics, is not a good idea because it releases harmful gases into the atmosphere.

Landfills and incineration have worked well for a long time. However, environmental scientists do not believe they have much of a future. Older landfills are already causing damage to surrounding **ecosystems**. The gases produced as garbage breaks down are called **greenhouse gases**.

Recycling

One solution to the planet's garbage problem is recycling. Recycling usually means taking waste material such as metal, glass, plastic, and paper and turning it into something useful. It does not mean turning it into exactly the same material—this is often too complicated and expensive. The goal is to recycle waste into products that would otherwise use up valuable resources. Besides reducing the amount of trash that is discarded, the greatest benefit of recycling is that it saves energy compared to making things that are brand new. It also creates lots of new jobs.

There are some people who think recycling is a bad idea. They argue that the extra fuel used to collect and transport recyclable material does its own harm. Another argument against recycling is that it takes jobs away from people who work in industries such as lumber and mining.

Studies in Europe and the United States show that recycling is the best way to dispose of household waste roughly 80 percent of the time. The fact is that for recycling to be worthwhile, the entire process has to work from start to finish. That includes knowing that there are consumers for recycled products. If no one buys recycled products, they just get thrown away!

Workers sort through plastic and glass bottles at a recycling plant.

They smell bad, are unhealthy to breathe, and contribute to climate change after they enter the atmosphere.

Landfill gases are created by the microorganisms that eat the trash. They cannot be contained, and sometimes they actually explode, causing great damage to nearby areas. Laws were passed in the United States during the 1990s to force landfill operators to collect and control gases and dispose of them safely. In some places, these gases are burned off in ways that produce energy.

The bigger problem is when landfill gases contaminate the groundwater beneath them. These contaminants include dozens of chemicals that can make living things sick. In neighborhoods near some older landfills, cancer rates are much higher than normal. It is difficult to prove a link scientifically, but that doesn't make the people living in these neighborhoods feel any safer.

People have been incinerating garbage since ancient times. But scientists are wondering how much longer we can continue this. When trash is burned—especially if it is not properly sorted beforehand—it releases toxic substances into the air.

Burning trash also produces ash. In **commercial** incinerators, there are two types of ash. Bottom ash settles at the bottom of the incinerator. It is scraped out and used to make roads and concrete blocks. Fly ash floats up during the burning process. In most developed countries, laws dictate

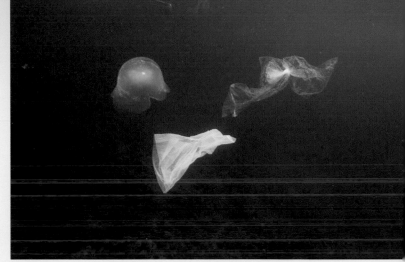

A jellyfish and a plastic bag look very similar underwater, which is a big problem for sea turtles. Can you tell which is which?

that it must be captured. That's because fly ash can be harmful when it enters the atmosphere. Among other things, it contains substances that are known to damage the lungs. In the United States, environmental scientists want tougher laws to control fly ash.

WATER PROBLEMS

Unfortunately, much of what we throw away ends up in rivers and oceans. In fact, at least 80 percent of the garbage in the world's oceans starts as trash that was discarded on land. This includes items that fall off of garbage barges—some of which is already contaminated. For people, trash in the water is ugly and **unsanitary**. For animals and marine life, what we throw away can be deadly.

For example, many species of sea turtles feed on jellyfish. In the open ocean, they cannot always tell the difference between a jellyfish and a plastic bag you get at the grocery store. And because the throats of sea turtles are built to keep jellyfish from wriggling away, once they begin to swallow a bag, it may get stuck.

SPACE TRASH

If there were one place that seemed "safe" to throw things away, it would be outer space, right? Wrong. The U.S. Department of Defense tracks more than 20,000 pieces of junk orbiting our planet. Some space trash—leftover material from rockets and satellites launched into orbit—travels at 25,000 miles per hour (40,000 kilometers per hour). At that speed, even a tiny screw can destroy a valuable communications satellite or, worse, part of the International Space Station.

When space trash is drawn by gravity into the earth's atmosphere, it burns up before it hits the ground. In that sense, it cleans up after itself. The problem is that there is more garbage being created in earth's orbit than is burning up. In 2010, a U.S. satellite slammed into a Russian satellite. It was the first time two large objects ever struck each other in space. The result? More than 1,500 "new" pieces of space trash to keep track of!

This image illustrates how space trash hovers above and around the earth.

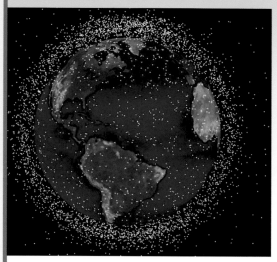

Another way we throw things away is when we flush the toilet. When a person takes medicine or prescription drugs, a small amount leaves the body each time that person goes to the bathroom. The wastewater travels to sewage treatment plants, which remove contaminants so that it can be released into the environment.

But these plants don't get rid of 100 percent of the chemicals in the water. That can be a problem for fish, including small, shiny species known as minnows. If you have ever gone fishing, you might have used a minnow as bait. In 2008, the **Environmental Protection Agency** reported that several different medicines were showing up in fish species, including minnows. Traces of the same medicines were also found in larger fish that eat minnows. These chemicals cause abnormal growths in fish. Sadly, in some places, minnows might not survive.

GARBAGE ON THE DINNER TABLE

Over the past decade, scientists have noticed that what we throw away may end up back in the food we eat. Indeed, a class of chemicals called **polybrominated diphenyl ethers (PBDEs)** has started showing up in everything from fish to butter to mother's milk. When PBDEs enter the human body, they affect the thyroid. This is especially dangerous for nursing infants. Recent evidence shows that toddlers exposed to high levels of PBDEs as babies scored lower on early IQ tests than toddlers who had not been exposed.

PBDEs have been used for decades as a flame retardant in foam cushions, computer cases, car dashboards, and other everyday products. When these products are thrown away and begin to break down, the PBDEs enter the environment through the ground water and also as dust particles in the air. Many countries banned the use of PBDEs. In the United States, several states have done the same, and a lot of companies simply stopped using them. Unfortunately, these chemicals are probably coming from trash we threw away a generation ago.

WORLD VIEW

Recycling is a great way to protect the environment. One thing it does is limit the amount of trash that ends up in landfills. Recycling also sustains many life forms in nature. For example, paper and cardboard products are made from trees. By recycling these materials, you can help forests grow bigger and stronger.

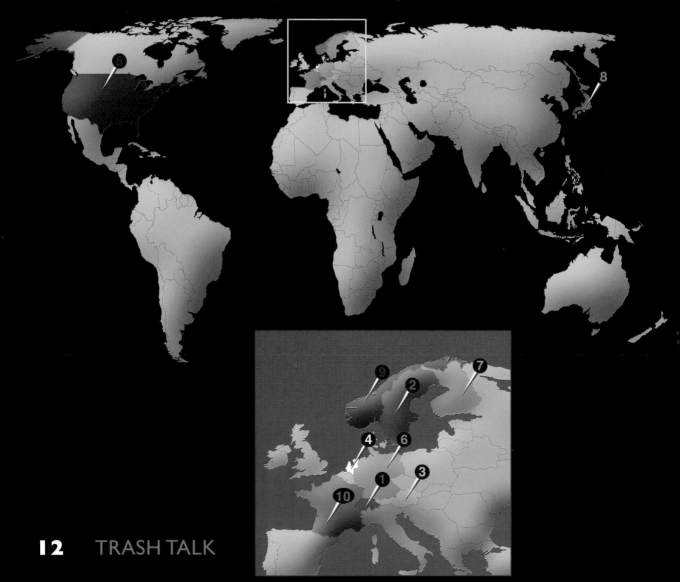

Top Ten Paper Recycling Countries

According to this chart, the average American recycles nearly 320 pounds (0.15 tonnes*) of paper each year.

PRODUCTION PER 1,000 PEOPLE

	COUNTRY	TONNES	POUNDS
1	Switzerland	167.36	368,965
2	Sweden	164.61	362,902
3	Austria	157.77	347,823
4	Netherlands	155.30	342,377
5	United States	144.14	317,774
6	Germany	140.55	309,859
7	Finland	134.80	297,183
8	Japan	116.55	256,948
9	Norway	98.26	216,626
10	France	93.62	206,396

A tonne is equivalent to 2,205 pounds.

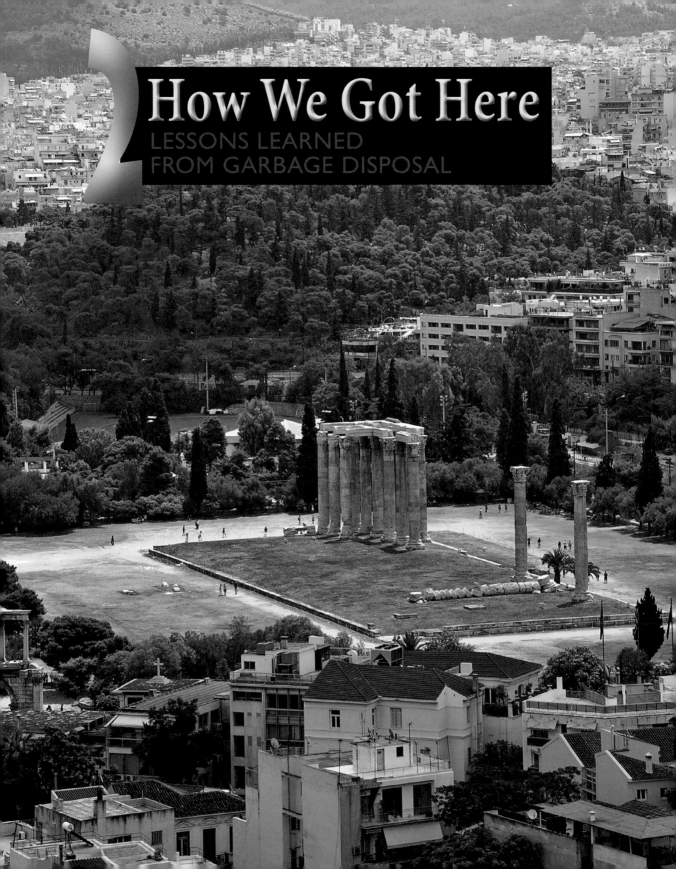

How We Got Here

LESSONS LEARNED FROM GARBAGE DISPOSAL

When archaeologists study early humans, they can tell a lot about how people lived from what they threw away. In more recent times, looking at *how* people threw things away tells us a lot, too. Garbage first became a problem about 2,500 years ago. By then, several large cities had been built. People lived and worked close together. Throwing trash out the back door into the street was not acceptable. The first city dump was in Athens, Greece. It was located outside the city gates. Some people had to carry their trash a mile or more to reach it. History's first "garbage men" made their appearance in Rome, Italy. They hauled away trash in carts starting around 200 B.C.

In smaller towns and villages, people continued to throw their trash into open ditches and bodies of water. They "recycled" what they could; pigs and dogs were often fed rotting food. The rest went into great heaps. This method of garbage disposal had two drawbacks. First, it smelled horrible. Second, it contributed to diseases and **epidemics**.

Athens is one of the world's most historic and beautiful cities. It was also the first to take trash disposal seriously.

The Great Blizzard

In New York City, it took a deadly snowstorm to create a modern **sanitation** department. In March of 1888, a blizzard dumped snow on the city for 36 straight hours. When the storm finally ended, some drifts were 50 feet (15.2 meters) high. New Yorkers shoveled themselves out of their homes, dumping the snow into the streets. Traffic slowed to a crawl for a week!

The city hired a small army of shovelers and haulers to clear the streets. They did a great job removing the snow. There had been a sanitation department in New York since 1881, but not until the Great Blizzard did anyone realize that citywide trash removal was possible. Today, New Yorkers still see the link between sanitation and snow removal. When a big snowstorm hits, the city's garbage trucks are pressed into duty. Workers attach huge plow blades to the front of the trucks, which are used to clear the streets.

THE BLACK DEATH

Garbage piles are a breeding ground for rats. Centuries ago, living with rodents was simply a fact of life. People didn't care too much if rats ate their garbage—better that than eating their food. In the 1300s, people began dying in huge numbers in China and other parts of Asia. In some cities, a thousand or more people died every day. The cause was the bubonic plague, which was spread by fleas that lived on black rats. The more rats that lived near humans, the more fleas there were to infect people.

By the end of the 1300s, the bubonic plague had spread to North Africa and Europe. In Europe, it killed millions of people every year. It was called the Black Death. By the time it had run its course, half of Europe's population had died. The plague returned for brief

In this print from Europe in the 1700s, people burn clothes infected with the Black Death.

periods in England, France, Russia, and Italy. Each time, poor sanitary conditions contributed to the disease.

Trash also played a role in two of history's most deadly diseases—typhoid and cholera. Although these **bacterial** illnesses are spread by contaminated water, garbage piles contributed greatly to the problem. The **microbes** and **parasites** that serve as carriers for these and other diseases multiply in damp, steamy mounds of garbage. The first recorded typhoid epidemic occurred in Athens around 425 B.C. A generation later, Athenians began dumping their trash outside city walls. Was that a coincidence?

MAN WITH A PLAN

The first person to take waste management seriously was Edwin Chadwick. He was an English politician who was

This print from the 1800s depicts the scene as Edwin Chadwick (third from right) made his case for more sanitary conditions in England.

concerned with the working conditions of London's poor. After a typhoid epidemic swept through England in the 1830s, Chadwick was asked to investigate the role poor sanitation may have played. In 1842, he wrote a report called "The Sanitary Conditions of the Labouring Population." In it, Chadwick showed the link between disease and sanitary conditions. Six years later, the government created the Central Board of Health. It oversaw garbage collection, street cleaning, and wastewater.

Soon other major cities began to take their trash more seriously. A city is only as strong as its workers, and when workers get sick and die, then it is in everyone's interest to clean things up. Still, it took another 50 years before most cities had some kind of sanitation department.

England was also the birthplace of the first trash incinerator. Burning garbage was nothing new, of course. In rural areas, most people around the world disposed of their garbage this way. In cities, **methane** buildup in large dumps had caused roaring fires. However, in 1874, Steven Fryer invented the Destructor, an enormous furnace that burned anything placed inside it. Some of the heat created by the Destructor was used to create electricity. A decade later, a giant incinerator was constructed on Governor's Island to burn New York City's trash.

REUSE & RECYCLE

There is an old saying that one person's trash is another's treasure. That has been true for centuries. What some people think is useless junk, someone else is willing to repair and use again. In many developing countries, this is still the case. From South America to Africa to

For waste pickers, discarded electronic items are like a treasure trove.

Indonesia, "waste pickers" scour huge mounds of trash for items they can use or sell.

Sometimes these items include discarded electronics (also called e-waste) shipped out of Europe and North America. Waste pickers break old computers apart to collect components that can be used again. They also look for tiny bits of valuable metal, including gold and silver. Unfortunately, this exposes waste pickers to dangerous chemicals, including lead and mercury.

Some people get "reusing" confused with recycling. As most people know, recycling means using waste materials to create new materials or products. In this sense, recycling is less than 250 years old. Modern recycling started during the Industrial Revolution, when raw materials—especially metals—were needed in great quantities at the lowest possible price.

People saved and collected scraps of metal that could be sold to peddlers. In turn, the peddlers sold the metal to factories, where it was melted down and used to make new products. The railroad industry and later the automotive industry depended on this source of material. During times of war, when metal was needed for **ammunition**, recycling became a matter of national defense.

Recycling as we know it today really took off during the 1970s. The cost of energy rose quickly during this decade. Suddenly it made sense to recycle glass, paper, plastic, and metal. For example, it takes 95 percent less energy to make recycled aluminum than new aluminum. People liked the idea of recycling. Businesses eventually embraced it, too. Recycling helped them save money and do something good for the environment.

HISTORY OF LANDFILLS

There are roughly 3,000 active landfills in the United States. Many people believe that the famous Marina District in San Francisco, California, was built on America's oldest landfill. However, this is not the case. The Marina District was built on top of rubble from the 1906 earthquake, along with mud dredged from San Francisco Bay. It was never used as a garbage dump.

The first U.S. landfill was in California—about three hours away, in Fresno. Trash was compacted and buried there on a daily basis starting in 1937. The landfill closed in 1989, after tests showed evidence of methane and other gases in the water wells of nearby residents. It was declared a Superfund clean-up site, meaning the government recognized it was highly contaminated. In one of the strangest twists in the history of trash, the Fresno Municipal Sanitary Landfill was declared a National Historic Landmark in 2001.

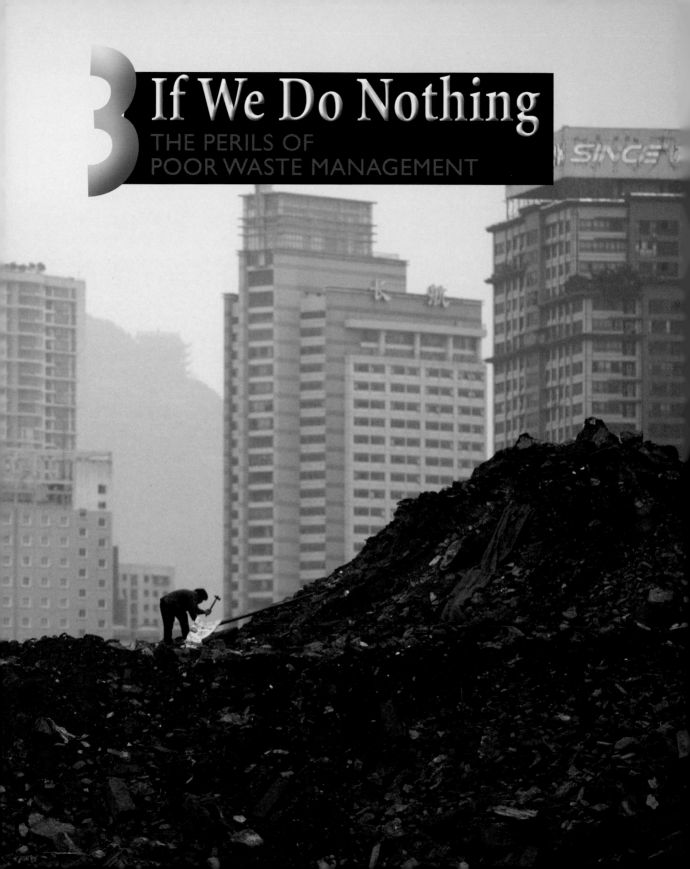

3 If We Do Nothing

THE PERILS OF POOR WASTE MANAGEMENT

The math of garbage is scary. Humans are producing more garbage than ever, and we are running out of places to put it. What happens when we simply have too much? Hopefully, that point will never come. Unfortunately, some believe we are already there. In China, for example, more than 8 billion tons of trash pile up each year. At that rate, every landfill near China's major cities will be full by 2020.

When a city of a million or more people has nowhere left to put its trash, the result can be an environmental catastrophe. It may have to create new landfills in sensitive natural areas. In developing countries, there is little choice but to let the trash pile up. When millions of poor people live and work near growing mountains of garbage, the chance for disease to develop and spread increases, too. Their daily struggle will become even harder.

A worker looks for recyclable materials at a construction site in China. The country produces a staggering amount of garbage every year.

AIR TRASH

Have you ever wondered how much trash airlines have to deal with? The average passenger creates 1.3 pounds (0.6 kilograms) of wastepaper alone on every flight. About three-quarters of the trash left on airplanes is recyclable. Yet, in 2010, industry estimates showed airlines recycle just 20 percent of their garbage. How much garbage are we talking about? During the first 10 years of the 21st century, the number of aluminum cans the world's airlines discarded instead of recycling could have been used to build more than 500 new planes!

The only good alternative is to send trash farther away. But moving garbage from the places people live to the places they don't is an expensive solution. With fuel costs rising, it will continue to get more expensive. And the energy needed to move tons of trash over long distances can do further damage to the environment in the form of pollution.

Politicians, business people, and scientists agree that it will take creative thinking to solve the problem of trash in cities. They understand the solution will involve more efficient recycling and perhaps a way to turn waste into clean energy. These approaches take a long time to perfect. And so far only a few companies have developed ideas that might work.

THE TERZIGNO DILEMMA

The garbage problem can be particularly bad in Europe. The city of Naples in Italy is one of the most beautiful in the world. From the highest points you can see the romantic Isle of Capri and towering Mt. Vesuvius, which

Trash piled up on roads and sidewalks is a common sight in Naples.

looms above the ancient ruins of Pompeii. You can also see (and sometimes smell) the Cava Sari landfill in Terzigno, just to the east. Terzigno is where Naples puts its garbage. Companies are allowed to dump their toxic waste as well. Those who live nearby experience itchy skin, sore throats, and stomach aches. People keep their windows shut, and children are not allowed to play outside.

The Cava Sari landfill is overflowing. The people of Terzigno were looking forward to the day when it finally closes. They were shocked when they heard a new landfill would soon be opened nearby. They took to the streets in angry protest and burned some garbage trucks. Garbage pickup was halted in Naples. Within a couple of days, the city was overrun with trash. This pointed out another problem. People in Naples only recycle five percent of their garbage! If anyone questions what would happen if a city is held prisoner by its own garbage problem, Naples may be the answer.

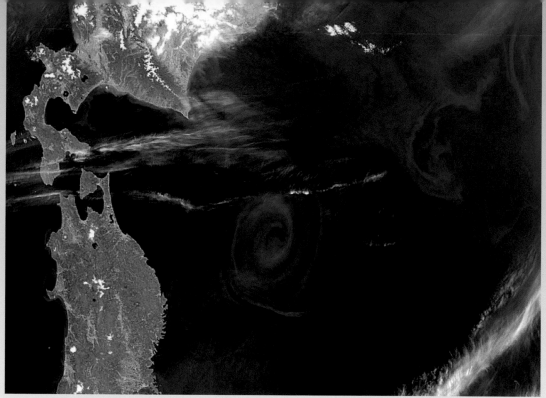

Seen from space as a swirl in the ocean, the Great Pacific Garbage Patch threatens Japan (top left), the United States, and the waters between them.

GARBAGE PATCH

If you spend enough time flying over the world's oceans, you are bound to see some jaw-dropping sights. None, however, is as amazing or disgusting as the Great Pacific Garbage Patch. All told, the patch covers an area larger than the state of Texas.

This "floating island" of marine **debris** is trapped in the North Pacific Gyre, which also happens to be the world's largest ecosystem. The Gyre is formed by four currents that cover about 20 million square miles (51.8 million square kilometers). These currents pull plastic and other floating material from the coasts of Japan and North America. It takes about six years for a soda bottle tossed into the ocean in California to join the Great Pacific Garbage Patch.

But it's not what you can see of the patch that is damaging the ecosystem. It's what you can't. Plastic breaks down over a period of years, turning into smaller and smaller pieces. These little flakes float at or near the surface of the water and underneath and between the larger pieces of trash. The larger pieces, meanwhile, can serve as rafts for invasive species.

The great danger to the marine environment has to do with the tiny pieces of plastic. As they break down, they attract pollutants that already exist in seawater. Over the course of many years, these pollutants become very concentrated on the plastic bits. Birds and fish mistake them for tiny sea creatures and eat them. These substances collect inside them, disrupting their body chemistry.

When we catch and eat these sea creatures, those chemicals pass into our bodies. The next time you miss a wastebasket with a snack wrapper or let a bottle cap roll away, think about where it may end up one day...in you!

UNSTABLE

When trash piles up, it sometimes comes crashing down. The city of Sidon, Lebanon is one of the most beautiful on the Mediterranean Sea. In 1982, Sidon was occupied by Israeli forces. After they left, rubble from the buildings that were destroyed was piled up a few miles outside of town. After that, the town kept piling garbage there. In 2008, a minor earthquake and a rainstorm caused part of the Sidon dump to collapse. It slid into the sea, fouling the entire Lebanese coast. Some of Sidon's garbage floated all the way to Cyprus and Greece.

Bright Ideas

FINDING CREATIVE WAYS TO USE TRASH

Most people look at the planet's garbage situation and wonder if there is any hope. Thanks to a lot of clever people who are working on this problem, it looks like there is. Some scientists and engineers are developing ways to harness biomass as an energy source. Biomass is a term for organic material that can be used for fuel. Any garbage that is not metal, plastic, or synthetic might be a good source of biomass. This includes food, wood chips, and plants. For example, a discarded hamburger could be considered biomass.

Fuel made from biomass is called biofuel. The power created by biofuel is called bioenergy. Right now, corn is the source of most biofuel. The problem is that it takes almost as much energy to produce the corn as the corn creates. Also, since living things need corn for food, the hope is to find other types of biomass, including different types of grasses, parts of plants that aren't eaten (such as corn husks), and even tree trimmings and lawn clippings.

A scientist examines a container of biomass. Researchers are working to find ways to turn garbage into biofuel.

MAKING ETHANOL

When biomass is allowed to **ferment**, the sugars are eaten by microorganisms. The waste product they produce is ethanol. Ethanol is a highly flammable fuel that can be used efficiently in most types of engines. Because ethanol burns cleaner and does not have to be taken from deep in the earth, it is a good alternative energy source. Also, the byproducts of ethanol can be used in cattle feed.

In 2007, the United States government awarded $385 million to six bioenergy companies to develop fuels from biomass. According to scientists, one day it may be possible for biofuels to replace up to 4 billion barrels of crude oil a year. That is about two-thirds of the oil Americans use now.

With advances in biofuels and bioenergy, there could come a time when almost every bit of what we throw away will be put to good use. Our garbage will be sorted into organic and inorganic categories. Organic material will be used to create energy. Inorganic material will be recycled into new products. Besides making the planet a better place to live, "bio-industries" will provide millions of new jobs

The Crystal Lake Ski Area in Wisconsin was built on ground that used to be a landfill.

for people in every part of the world. At the end of the day, there will be little or no trash to talk about.

NEW TAKES ON TRASH

Until that day comes, people have to deal with the reality of our garbage. Fortunately, they are doing so in smart ways. Back in 1999, the countries of Europe got together and agreed to change the way they managed their landfills. They understood that no matter how well a landfill is designed, one day it will fail. Their "Landfill Directive" stated that all trash—household, business, and industrial—had to be "pretreated" before it could go into the ground. Since 2001, almost every landfill in the European Union has followed this rule. This has had a positive impact on the quality of the surface water, groundwater, soil, and air all over Europe.

Plasma Arc Incinerators

Some countries are experimenting with a new type of incineration that uses super-hot plasma. High-voltage electricity is passed between two electrodes, which creates an arc. Gas passes through this arc—and is heated to thousands of degrees—before it enters a chamber containing garbage. At these temperatures, waste is broken down into atoms.

The advantage of Plasma Arc technology is that it produces very little air pollution. After the waste is superheated, the gases left over are removed from the chamber. They can be used to run the incinerator or sold to other industries as fuel. There are several Plasma Arc incinerators in use in Asia and Canada. So far, none are big enough to handle all the garbage a major city produces. However, Los Angeles is planning to build one in the future.

The importance of improving landfills is easier to see when you actually stand in front of the gigantic mound created by one. The Fresh Kills landfill in Staten Island, New York, began as a temporary dump in the 1940s. Soon it became the main dump for New York City. By the 1990s, it was one of the largest manmade structures on earth. In 2009, the city announced plans to transform the landfill into a park. The project will take 30 years. Environmental scientists have been part of the planning process. The hope is that this land—which is three times larger than Manhattan's Central Park—can be enjoyed without damage to people or the environment.

Sometimes what seems like a smart solution to the planet's garbage problem isn't smart at all. While most people look up at the stars in awe and wonder, others see the next great "landfill." Why, they ask, can't we launch our trash into space? It's an interesting idea. Heap our garbage onto rockets, aim them toward the sun, and then let the trash go once it has left earth's atmosphere. The waste would continue traveling through space until it burned up. So what's the problem? Right now it would simply be too expensive. Rocket launches cost a lot of money. To send our garbage to the sun would cost trillions of dollars a day.

When scientists at the Japanese Aerospace Exploration Agency (JAEA) look to the sky, they see something else. Today, we depend heavily on satellites for information and communication. But all that space junk orbiting the earth will become a problem. In 2011, the JAEA announced that it was working with a fishing net company to make a gigantic metal net. The net will be launched into orbit and then fill itself with debris. Gravity will then pull it back into the atmosphere, where the space trash will harmlessly burn up.

TRASH ART

During the Great Depression of the 1930s, creative people supported themselves in **ingenious** ways. Out-of-work artists took discarded wooden boxes, picture frames, popsicle sticks, and other scraps of wood and created "Tramp Art." They would sell their works or trade them for food. Now Tramp Art has become very valuable. Some pieces sell for thousands of dollars.

There are still people who look at trash and see a work of art. Today artists have a lot more material to work with. Between discarded electronics and the many shapes and textures of plastic, they can let their imaginations run wild. At any given time, somewhere in a major city, art lovers are oohing and aahing as they stand in a gallery looking at a work of art that was "saved" from the city dump.

5 Trailblazers

These people are doing things to help clean up the world today...and make it a better place for tomorrow.

Tom Szaky

Business Owner

Szaky (left) is the founder of TerraCycle. His company collects hard-to-recycle items such as juice pouches, pens, and toothbrushes and turns them into backpacks, pencil cases, and park benches. He hopes every country will use this system one day.

Paijit Sangchai

Scientist

In Sangchai's native Thailand, coated paper—the kind used for menus and packaging—was being burned instead of recycled. Sangchai knew there had to be a better way. He discovered a technique to combine **enzymes** to eat away the coating so almost all of the paper can be recycled.

Richard Fuller
Environmental Engineer

Fuller (right) started the Blacksmith Institute in New York City to help control the world's pollution problems. Among other things, the organization looks for simple, inexpensive ways to clean up soil that has been contaminated by garbage and industrial waste. Working in small villages and city slums, Blacksmith has used worms and molasses to get the job done.

William McDonough & Michael Braungart
Authors

In their book *Cradle to Cradle*, McDonough and Braungart showed how businesses can reduce the amount of waste they create—and still make a profit. The book was printed on "paper"…sort of. It was actually made of recycled plastic that feels like paper!

LEFT: Tom Szaky   **ABOVE**: Richard Fuller

6 Field Tested

andfills are not normally places you think of as wildlife habitats. However, in California's Santa Clara County, scientists and **conservationists** teamed up to turn a landfill into a home for a threatened insect species. The bay checkerspot butterfly was once abundant on the San Francisco Peninsula, but it began to disappear in the 1980s. People saw a chance to do a good thing and help the bay checkerspot survive.

The problem was that invasive species of plants had replaced those that the bay checkerspot depended on. At one point, scientists could find populations of the butterfly in only five places, including Kirby Canyon. The owner of a landfill there agreed to help create a preserve and fund research into the bay checkerspot. When sections of the landfill were full, the company grew the species of plants the butterfly needed for food and breeding.

The bay checkerspot lives up to 10 days after emerging from its cocoon. If it suffers any kind of environmental stress, its population will decline rapidly. Fortunately, researchers believe this won't happen. Not all landfills are such good neighbors. Scientists hope more will follow the lead of Kirby Canyon, because losing any species can have a major effect on an ecosystem.

The bay checkerspot butterfly was dying out until the owner of a landfill worked with the local community to save it.

Career Opportunities

WORKING TO MANAGE OUR WASTE

Saying you work in garbage does not sound very glamorous. Does it sound better to say you solved the planet's most pressing problem? That is the challenge that lies ahead for the bright, motivated, hard-working people who want to turn trash talk into trash action.

Unlike waste management jobs of old, future jobs in this industry will focus on finding clever ways *not* to bury and burn what we throw away. That will almost certainly involve turning trash into energy and products people need. Employers will be looking for workers with a wide range of talents and interests. These include all branches of science and engineering, as well as expertise in managing time, money, people, and resources.

A worker cleans up globs of oil after the 2010 disaster in the Gulf of Mexico. Jobs in waste management are some of the most important in the world.

CREATING NEW JOBS

There are other jobs that will become crucial in getting a handle on our garbage problems. For example, recycling works best when it produces material for things that people want or need. That means inventors and product designers will be in great demand. They will work with recyclers to understand what kinds of materials are available and then think up cool things to make to improve the lives of millions of people.

Another important job in overcoming the world's trash challenges will be communicating with and educating people in different cultures. These jobs are perfect for **anthropologists** and **sociologists**, who may find themselves on the "front lines" of the war on trash. Whether it is showing people the recycled products they can use, or explaining how to fit recycling into their daily lives, it is crucial to understand how populations think and act.

Landscape architects and park designers should also find their services in demand in the years to come. As landfills close, many cities will want to restore these areas to a more natural state. That will allow people to enjoy them as parks and recreational spaces. Transforming these spaces will require experts from many fields—including environmental engineering and arboriculture (the study of trees and shrubs).

If I am elected...

Changing the way we deal with trash takes a change in attitudes and often a change in laws. That is why some of the most important work in solving our garbage problem will be done by politicians. This will be a big change from the past. Many of the problems we face today are the result of people in government who were too slow or timid to make important decisions about the environment. Soon they will be gone. Will you be one of the people to replace them?

In the United States, anyone can run for political office. Anyone can work on a politician's staff. It helps to have a background in law or political science, but often it is unnecessary. A good heart, a good mind, and commitment to change is just as important. Tomorrow's politicians will continue the work that has begun in solving the country's trash problems.

For example, right now laws for disposing of old computers and cell phones are different from state to state. This is a problem all politicians can agree on. Work has begun to create a national law to make sure toxic e-waste is disposed of responsibly.

Saving the environment from pollution is one issue that politicians usually agree on.

8 Expert Opinions

When the best minds talk about the world's trash problems, it's worth listening to what they say…

"This growing mountain of garbage and trash represents not only an attitude of indifference toward valuable natural resources, but also a serious economic and public health problem."
—*Jimmy Carter, former U.S. president, on the dangers of ignoring our garbage problem*

"There are so many environmental problems associated with paper-making. I thought I should do something about it."
—*Paijit Sangchai, scientist, on how he found a way to recycle coated paper*

"There could be a charge or tax for any type of nonreusable shopping bag."
—*Benjamin Miller, garbage historian, on one way to reduce the number of plastic bags we throw away*

"We've made some heroic efforts, but the earth as a whole is in worse shape today than 30 years ago."

—*Denis Hayes, environmental activist, on the need to do more to control pollution*

"We are studying the **feasibility** of collecting the trash and turning it into fuel, while educating the public to the enormity of the problem."

—*Tony Haymet, Director of the Scripps Institution of Oceanography, on the Great Pacific Garbage Patch*

"The space around earth is like a pigsty."

—*Paul Wallis, journalist, on the growing problem of space trash*

"It is no longer enough to manage waste and minimize the environmental impacts of its treatment. From now on, waste must be used as a resource."

—*Michel Gourvennec, waste management expert, on putting garbage to work*

LEFT: Jimmy Carter   **ABOVE**: Denis Hayes

9 What Can I Do?

The trash problem created by generations of ignorance and neglect will soon be the problem of your generation. You can start working on it right now. Use the resources at your disposal—the Internet, for example. This can be a powerful tool, especially if you want your voice to be heard. Educating people about the dangers of disposing of trash irresponsibly is a great way to reach out to others without creating your own trash.

You can send e-mails to support good causes. You can send e-mails to complain. A great way to make a difference is to contact companies that you believe are using too much packaging for their products. Tell them you like what they make, but point out that your family would continue to buy from them without all the fancy packaging.

Composting is another good idea. Starting a compost heap is easy. You can do it in your backyard. Some people use specially designed crates to compost, but these devices aren't absolutely necessary. The key is to keep your compostable material covered and moist. After a few weeks, you can transfer it to a garden or lawn. Your flowers, plants, and grass will thank you! And so will our planet, because you'll be limiting the amount of trash you produce.

You would be surprised by the number of products that are compostable, including this man's cell phone case.

Glossary

Ammunition—Bullets and other items fired from guns.

Anthropologists—People who study humans and their evolution.

Bacterial—Caused by single-celled microorganisms that live in soil, water, or bodies of plants and animals.

Biodegradable—Capable of being broken down into materials that don't harm the environment.

Climate Change—A long-term change in weather conditions.

Commercial—Owned by a business.

Conservationists—People who preserve and protect the environment.

Debris—Another term for waste or trash.

Ecosystems—All the organisms, plants, and animals that make up specific ecological areas.

Environmental Protection Agency—The government agency in the United States charged with protecting the environment.

Enzymes—Proteins produced by living cells that create or speed up various types of reactions.

Epidemics—Outbreaks of disease that affect many people and spread quickly.

Feasibility—The capability of being done.

Ferment—The chemical breakdown of a substance that produces gases.

Greenhouse Gases—Gases that trap heat in the atmosphere, just as a greenhouse does during the winter.

Incineration—Disposing of material by burning it.

Ingenious—Clever and smart.

Methane—A colorless and odorless gas that is also flammable.

Microbes—Another term for microorganisms or germs.

Organic—Produced naturally, without the help of pesticides or chemical fertilizers.

Parasites—Organisms that live by feeding off of other living things.

Polybrominated Diphenyl Ethers (PBDEs)—Chemical compounds that are used in a variety of products, including electronics and plastics.

Sanitation—The maintenance of clean living conditions.

Sociologists—People who study societies and behavior.

Unsanitary—Dirty and unhealthy.

Sources

The authors relied on many different books, magazines, and organizations to do research for this book. Listed below are the primary sources of information and their websites:

The Associated Press	www.ap.org
Discover Magazine	www.discovermagazine.com
Federal News Service	www.fnsg.com
International Herald Tribune	www.global.nytimes.com
National Geographic Magazine	www.nationalgeographic.com.
The New York Times	www.nytimes.com
Newsweek Magazine	www.newsweek.com
Science Magazine	www.sciencemag.org
Seattle Post-Intelligencer	www.seattlepi.com
Time Magazine	www.time.com

Resources

To get involved with efforts to help the environment, you can contact these organizations:

Environmental Protection Agency	www.epa.gov/recyclecity
EnvironmentalChemistry.com	www.environmentalchemistry.com
National Geographic Kids	www.kids.nationalgeographic.com
National Institute of Environmental Health	www.niehs.nih.gov
Zero Waste America	www.zerowasteamerica.org

For more information on the subjects covered in this book:

Burns, Loree Griffin. *Tracking Trash: Flotsam, Jetsam, and the Science of Ocean Motion.* San Anselmo, California. Sandpiper Press, 2010.

Gates, Alexander. *Encyclopedia of Pollution: Air, Earth, and Water.* New York, New York. Facts on File, 2011.

Miller, Debra A. *Garbage and Recycling.* San Diego, California. Lucent Books, 2009.

Rogers, Heather. *Gone Tomorrow: The Hidden Life of Garbage.* New York, New York. The New Press, 2006.

Index

Page numbers in **bold** refer to illustrations.

The Authors

AMY K. TILMONT is a science teacher at The Rumson Country Day School in Rumson, New Jersey. She is a graduate of Lycoming College. Her areas of expertise include Geology and Environmental Science.

JEFFREY R. GARSIDE is also a science teacher at The Rumson Country Day School. He graduated from Northeastern University and holds a Masters degree from Kean College. Jeff teaches Chemistry, Physics and Biology, and is head of RCDS's Science Department.

MARK STEWART has written more than 200 non-fiction books for the school and library market. He has an undergraduate degree in History from Duke University. Mark's work in environmental studies includes books on the plants and animals of New York (where he grew up) and New Jersey (where he lives now).